# Divine Interventions
*Inspired By God*

Stadene Campbell

Divine Interventions: Inspired by God
©2022 Stadene Campbell

All Rights Reserved. This book is protected by the copyright laws of the United States of America. This book may not be copied or reprinted for commercial gain or profit. The use of short quotations or occasional page copying for personal, or group study is permitted and encouraged. Permission will be granted upon request. For information regarding permission, write to Gift From Above Publishing, 501 Lisa St Suite 7A, Rincon, GA 31326.

Unless otherwise stated, all Scripture quotes are from the King James Version, Public Domain.

Published by Gift From Above Publishing
501 Lisa St Suite 7A
Rincon, GA 31326

**ISBN 979-8-218-03563-1**

Cover Design: Jeffrey (Jaebars) Townsell

Printed in the USA.

# Table of Contents

ACKNOWLEDGMENT.................................................................... 5

INTRODUCTION ......................................................................... 8

DO YOU SEE YOURSELF AS A SMALL AXE?.................................10

AN UGLY DUCKLING OR A SWAN................................................15

CAN A LEOPARD CHANGE ITS SPOTS? .........................................20

A PSALM 91 INSPIRATION..........................................................25

ISN'T THAT THE CARPENTER'S SON? ..........................................31

KNOW DISTRACTIONS AND SAY NO! TO DISTRACTIONS .............36

IS YOUR PAST PASSED?..............................................................41

SNOW WHITE ...........................................................................46

THEY COULD HAVE, BUT THEY COULDN'T... ...............................52

THE SEPARATION IS PREPARATION FOR PROMOTION ................57

DON'T FOCUS ON THE PROCESS.................................................63

WATCH OUT FOR THE PRODUCT... .............................................63

GOD'S PUPPET!.........................................................................69

HE ALONE SHOULD PULL OUR STRINGS. ....................................69

NAME BRAND / ........................................................................74

BRAND NAME ..........................................................................74

JUST ONE STONE.......................................................................80

A SPIRITUAL MRI.......................................................................85

UNCTION TO FUNCTION ...........................................................90

| | |
|---|---|
| PLEASING EVERYBODY | 96 |
| THE BOY WHO CRIED WOLF/SOUNDING THE TRUMPET | 101 |
| PLANTED NOT BURIED | 107 |
| ADORN/ ENHANCE SELF | 112 |
| STRANGE ADDICTIONS | 118 |
| A BROKEN PENCIL | 124 |
| WHAT ARE YOUR THOUGHTS? | 129 |
| JEALOUSY, A BIG KILLER | 135 |
| YOU ARE LIGHT! | 141 |
| SEED SOWERS | 146 |
| STONE THROWERS | 151 |
| LIVING AMONG THE TOMBS, IT SEEMS | 157 |
| YOU ARE AN IMPORTANT MEMBER | 164 |
| REJECTED – | 170 |
| NOW NEEDED… | 170 |
| DIFFERENT SEASONS… | 175 |
| DIFFERENT TIMES | 175 |
| ABOUT THE AUTHOR | 181 |

# *Acknowledgment*

First, I must acknowledge the Most High God, my Heavenly Father, my guide, and my inspiration. Without Him, it could not be possible as all my inspirations come from the Holy Spirit. I give Him all the glory. When He would have me up late at night, downloading in my spirit while I write, I understand, and now I can genuinely say Thank you, Lord Jesus.

I would love to say a big thank you to my Senior Pastor, Rebecca Stewart (Servant), who did not doubt. She believed in me and encouraged me to continue this endeavor. Servant, like the mother I no longer have, constantly pushes me to go forth and see what I didn't see in myself. Thank you for the prayers and for staying up with me while working on God's book.

Some believed in me right from the beginning:
  ★My Armor Bearer Kensha Felicien, who stands with me in everything.

★ Chaplain Yvonne Hall, for her encouragement and corrections on specific ideas. Thank you for introducing me to my Publisher and investing in this book.

★ To my son, Shaniel Thompson, for always cheering on his mom and complimenting my growth.

★ Missionary Una Edwards, who kept the prayers blazing and made sure I was well maintained and covered.

★ Chaplain Lecia Lindsay, our church secretary, who always answered and delivered on a call, your time and faithfulness is well appreciated.

★ Pastor Gail London-Lewis, for her encouraging words and prayers.

Let's not forget Aunty Andrea Joseph, who helped with the title while following the leading of the Holy Ghost. That day, we sat discussing the book, and the Holy Ghost intervened; it was awesome.

To my entire church family, this could not have felt so accomplished. Thank you for always rooting for me even when I went through challenges. The continuous prayers, texts, etc. were well received, so once again, I say a big Thank you.

I also want to thank everyone who has been a part of my journey during this walk of life. Whether you believed in me or not, you were all a part of my process. I thank God for you all. I had some experiences in life which I can now look back on and say HALLELUJAH! THANK YOU, JESUS! For the journey which led me to where I am today. Through overcoming these experiences, I can encourage others who are still a captive of their past or those living a life without Christ.

My acknowledgment would not be complete without thanking the team at Gift From Above Publishing with Publisher Natasha Tingman. Thank you for your patience and time in making this a huge success.

# *Introduction*

This book is composed of inspirational passages created to inspire and change lives for the Glory of God through the Holy Spirit. The passages are based on fictional stories, which I had the pleasure of reading during my earlier stages of life. Yet, revealed to me by the Holy Spirit, they are actual happenings replaced with fictional characters, and their realities are overlooked. They coincide with everyday situations and are linked with scriptures from the Word of God to speak to a society destined for greatness by the hands of Almighty God. People who are hurting, depressed, abused, and suffer from low self-esteem, are beneficiaries of the contents of this book. All revelations are from the Holy Spirit, and it's promising to do better than a regular therapy session. Some of these inspirations were factors of my own healing and ways of overcoming life's hurdles.

Readers are expected to gain self-confidence, growth, and healing of past hurts while seeing life in a more positive light through God's words. As stated in the book of Hebrews, Chapter 4:10, "the word of God is quick and powerful...."

Be inspired as you read; may you have a divine encounter, and may divine intervention take place in your situations.

Be Blessed!

# Day 1

# Do You See Yourself as a Small Axe?

*"Therefore David ran, and stood upon the Philistine, and took his sword, and drew it out of the sheath thereof, and slew him, and cut off his head therewith. And when the Philistines saw their champion was dead, they fled."*

*~1 Samuel 17:51*

There is a saying in the Jamaican culture that states, "small axe falls big trees." This statement is factual and is very powerful if taken in the correct context. The hands which control the axe are also very significant.

You may see yourself as a small axe and often question your importance or your effectiveness, but be reminded that as an axe, you have the ability to take down a huge tree. It's not your size that counts but your content. In 1 Samuel 17, there was a shepherd boy named David, and he was the youngest and smallest of his brothers. Even though he was small in stature, there was a time when David's nation was faced with a crisis in which the Philistines (who were the enemies) had decided to come up against them. When the army of soldiers, who were looked upon to defend their country, got cold feet, David stood up to the mightiest of the enemy (Goliath) and defeated him. Everyone was surprised by the outcome except for David, who knew it wasn't himself who *actually* did this great throw down, but the God who lived in him. David had no army skills, but he had God. At that point in life, he had been seen as a small axe, but in the hand of the Almighty God, he tore down a big tree.

You, too, like David, can be that axe and tear down the trees that stand in your way. Sometimes you may face giants in your lives and feel like you just want to give up - to the pressures and stresses of life. Be encouraged, and be reminded it's not your size but your content that matters. The Bible also said in 1 John 4:4, "Ye are of God, little children, and overcome them: because greater is He that is in you, than he that is in the world." This tells us that we can conquer anything if we have God inside us.

So, see yourself as a small axe, allow God to control your life, and now consider yourself significant.

## *Reflections:*

1. Are there any giants in your life that are causing you to fear?

_____

_____

_____

_____

_____

2. What trees are facing you?

_____

_____

_____

_____

_____

3. Do you see yourself as too small to confront your giant?

_____
_____
_____
_____
_____
_____
_____

4. As an axe, whose hand are you in?

_____
_____
_____
_____
_____
_____
_____

# Day 2

# An Ugly Duckling or A Swan...

*"If ye were of the world, the world would love his own: but because ye are not of the world, but I have chosen you out of the world, therefore the world hateth you."*

*~John 15:19*

There is a story told of the odd duckling in the herd. He was mocked, jeered, ridiculed, and rejected by those he considered his own. Those who he expected to receive love from the most were the ones who turned on him. He was so ashamed and confused as to why the unkind treatment. It became so unbearable at one point that he decided to run away and try living life alone. During this saddest, loneliest, and most stressful time of his life, he discovered his true self. He was not a duckling in reality, but all along, he was one of the most beautiful birds in existence; he was a swan.

Sometimes being different can lower our self-esteem and bring us to the lowest place in feelings if allowed. It's understandable, but it's definitely not an option. If we could come to the place where we can recognize the enemy's plan to keep us in a place that doesn't allow us to grow into what we are destined to become. We must acknowledge that we are different and separate ourselves from what, where, and to who we don't belong.

John 15:19 says, "If ye were of the world, the world would love his own: but because ye are not of the world, but I have chosen you out of the world, therefore the world hateth you." This means that in the world (among ducklings), we will be hated because we are different. Not to worry, though; we are classified in 1 Peter 2:9 as a chosen generation. The Bible states, "But ye *are* a chosen generation, a royal priesthood, an holy nation, a peculiar people; that ye should shew forth the praises of him who hath called you out of darkness into his marvelous light:" Therefore, it's for us to see ourselves as that which we truly are. We often find our true selves in rejection, as did the swan. So the next time you feel inferior or feel left out and that you don't belong, just remember that you may not be ugly or less than but seem odd because of the wrong associates. Identify your true self, discover your kind and appreciate life.

You are most comfortable when you become who you are destined to be. Be true to yourself.

### BE THAT SWAN!!!

# *Reflections:*

1. What caused you to see yourself as an ugly duckling?

_____

_____

_____

_____

_____

_____

2. How well did you handle your rejection?

_____

_____

_____

_____

_____

_____

3. Have you discovered the real you in God?

_____
_____
_____
_____
_____
_____

4. Have you now concluded that it's ok to be different?

_____
_____
_____
_____
_____
_____

# Day 3

# Can a Leopard Change its Spots?

---

*"Therefore if any man be in Christ, he is a new creature: old things are passed away; behold, all things are become new."*

*~2 Corinthians 5:17*

---

I remember people saying to me, "a leopard cannot change its spots," in response to me and others who have publicly declared a change of lifestyle. Knowing the negative aspects of one's life will always trigger doubts about being positively transformed. In the natural, it is factual that a leopard cannot change its spots. Yet, in the spiritual, a person, no matter how spotty they are in sin, can become spotless by the blood of Jesus Christ.

As we are not leopards but human beings created by the creator but fallen because of sin, everyone can change. John 3:16 tell us that because of the love of God, Jesus Christ came and made way for us to be clean. Sin is compared to spots, so imagine for every sin we commit, a spot is placed on us, oh how spotty we are. For some, there is no space left for us to receive another. However, thank God that these spots can disappear with the death, burial, and resurrection of Jesus Christ. 2 Corinthians 5:17 says, "Therefore if any man *be* in Christ, *he is* a new creature: old things are passed away; behold, all things are become new."

God can change you from whatever you may have been spotted with, drug addiction, alcohol, prostitution, murder, etc. He can transform you into greatness. Just as he did in the book of Acts with Saul, who became Paul, there can be total changes of spots. Jesus died, and his death is the ultimate price for our sins. When we accept him as our redeemer, his blood cleanses us and purifies us from our sins. So now we become no longer spotted and blemished but new creatures. Let anyone lie to you and state that you cannot change, for all things are possible with God.

# *Reflections:*

1. What mistakes are you stained with?

   _____

   _____

   _____

   _____

   _____

   _____

2. Are you able to count your spots?

   _____

   _____

   _____

   _____

   _____

   _____

3. When was the last time you examined yourself?

___

4. Have your spots lessened in any way since you last checked?

___

# Day 4

# A Psalm 91 Inspiration

*He that dwelleth in the secret place of the Most High Shall abide under the shadow of the Almighty. I will say of the LORD, He is my refuge and my fortress: My God; in him will I trust. Surely he shall deliver thee from the snare of the fowler, And from the noisome pestilence. He shall cover thee with his feathers, and under his wings shalt thou trust: His truth shall be thy shield and buckler. Thou shalt not be afraid for the terror by night; Nor for the arrow that flieth by day; Nor for the pestilence that walketh in darkness; Nor for the destruction that wasteth at noonday. A thousand shall fall at thy side, and ten thousand at thy right hand; But it shall not come nigh thee. Only with thine eyes shalt thou behold And see the reward of the wicked. Because thou hast made the LORD, which is my refuge, Even the most High, thy habitation; There shall no evil befall thee, Neither shall any plague come nigh thy dwelling. For he shall give his angels charge over thee, To keep thee in all thy ways. They shall bear thee up in their hands, Lest thou dash thy foot against a stone. Thou shalt tread upon the lion and adder: The young lion and the dragon shalt thou trample under feet. Because he hath set his love upon me, therefore will I deliver him: I will set him on high, because he hath known my name. He shall call upon me, and I will answer him: I will be with him in trouble; I will deliver him, and honour him. With long life will I satisfy him, And shew him my salvation.*

*~Psalm 91*

A person who spends time in God's presence constantly is covered by Him. His covenant is with those who abide with Him. We have to be consistent and faithful in our relationship with Him.

God is our safe space and our shelter, our covering. We can trust Him to rescue us from traps, to deliver us from sicknesses and diseases, to deliver us from evil spirits. His words are our shield and protection. With God, there is no fear of dangers. When all things around us are affected, we have a promise and a hope to remain safe. We will be but witnesses to the things that overtake our enemies.

When we put God first, above and beyond, it ensures that no evil or misfortune will affect us. His angels are appointed and assigned to carry us. We shall overcome and conquer the evil one.

God's love repays our love. He will always come through. He will put you above and not beneath (Deuteronomy 28:13).

Whenever we call on God, He will answer. He'll never leave us nor forsake us, and long life He will give. All we have to do is play our part by making an effort to stay with Him in all things.

# *Reflections:*

1. Are you constantly in God's presence? If not, when was the last time you spent time in His presence?

_____

_____

_____

_____

_____

2. How secure are you in Christ? Are you a beneficiary of His coverage?

_____

_____

_____

_____

_____

3. Do you trust God wholeheartedly with your life?

_____

_____

_____

_____

_____

_____


4. What makes you not so secure?

_____

_____

_____

_____

_____

_____

# Day 5

# Isn't that the Carpenter's Son?

*"Is not this the carpenter's son? is not his mother called Mary? and his brethren, James, and Joses, and Simon, and Judas? And his sisters, are they not all with us? Whence then hath this man all these things? And they were offended in him. But Jesus said unto them, A prophet is not without honour, save in his own country, and in his own house. And he did not many mighty works there because of their unbelief."*

~Matthew 13:55-58

There are times when we may have been stereotyped and less respected because of our family background and where we originated from. We perform to the best of our abilities to ensure we are effective. We may be realistically the best but.... It matters not how talented or gifted or anointed we may be; people will treat us with scan courtesy just because of our background. It can be frustrating when we get rated based on our family or roots, not on our abilities. To know we are never celebrated or congratulated is very discouraging. Jesus himself experienced it.

Let's take courage, be not dismayed, and continue to do the good you do because a reward is waiting with God (Matthew 5:12). Continue doing what you were purposed to do as God assigned you. It's God who chooses us and not man. Concentrate not on men's opinions but be obedient to the Most High. You might be a carpenter's son, a seamstress's daughter, a barmaid's son, or even a harlot's daughter. Still, it doesn't mean you can't be powerful or positively effective. It's not the earthly parents that determine your purpose but the Heavenly

Father. So yes, you are this person's child, but most importantly, you are the child of the Most High God. Be not limited by your roots.

# *Reflections:*

1. Ever done your best at something but received no recognition? What was that something?

_____
_____
_____
_____
_____
_____

2. How does your family history affect your life?

_____
_____
_____
_____
_____
_____

3. Are you discouraged by others' opinions of you? Why do you think that is so?

_____

_____

_____

_____

_____

_____

_____

# Day 6

# Know Distractions and Say No! to Distractions

*"My sheep hear my voice, and I know them, and they follow me:"*

*~John 10:27*

In this world, there are numerous distractions set up for those who have decided to walk as believers of Christ. Distractions are anything that prevents someone from giving their full attention to something else. Can you name a few distractions in this life? I sure can. There are numerous kinds, for example, the media, work, family, friends, and enemies. Yes, these can all be forms of distraction. See, the enemy (the devil) knows what or who to use to get to us. So there are times when even our own family members will start acting up. But, if we pause to realize, the Word of God has already prepared us for what lies ahead. The Word of God lets us know that we do not wrestle against flesh and blood (human) but against principalities, powers, and rulers of the darkness of this world and spiritual wickedness in high places (Ephesians 6:12); which means it's all a spiritual battle. If we remember and can understand this, so many of us would be less caught up in fights and discussions that only hurt each other and still no solution to problems.

Therefore, we are encouraged to know the enemy and his strategies. Peter 5:8 (KJV) states, "Be sober, be vigilant; because your adversary the devil, as a roaring lion, walketh about, seeking whom he may devour:" If we don't identify the distractions set by him, we will fall to them.

Joseph was a young man who feared God. He once was set up by his master's wife, who tried to seduce him to get him in her bed, but Joseph knew distractions and resisted and ran because he remembered his God (Genesis 39:7-12).

Like Joseph, we need to identify the distractions and say no to them. They come to keep us at a distance from God and separate us from the things promised unto us.

Matthew 14:22-31 gives a clear example of what happens in the time of our distractions. We see where Jesus called Peter to walk on water, and he was going well until the waves distracted him and he started to sink. The winds and waves distracted him briefly, and it caught him unaware. Whatever it is that keeps you from spending time with God or whatever causes you to turn your eyes off him is a distraction. Do the right thing and say No! to whatever wind, waves, or storm may come your way.

**Remember to
Just Stay Focused...**

# Reflections:

1. Identify the main distractions in your life and on your walk with God?

___

___

___

___

___

2. Are they strong enough to keep you from growing in Christ?

___

___

___

___

___

3. How well are you able to ignore these distractions?

_____

_____

_____

_____

_____

_____

4. Think of some strategies to keep you focused on your goal.

_____

_____

_____

_____

_____

# Day 7

# *Is your Past Passed?*

*"And it came to pass, when they had brought them forth abroad, that he said, Escape for thy life; look not behind thee, neither stay thou in all the plain; escape to the mountain, lest thou be consumed."*

*"But his wife looked back from behind him, and she became a pillar of salt."*

*~Genesis 19:17, 26*

Before, accepting Christ in our lives it's common and a norm for us as people to operate or behave in ways that are unpleasant to our memory when we transform to newness. We have done things that some of us are even too ashamed to repeat. But we all have sinned and fallen short of the glory of God (Romans 3:23). Therefore, no one can say they have been perfect their whole life. Some people were killers, drug addicts, alcoholics, liars, fornicators, idolaters, etc. there are numerous names that we have been known as. However, our Heavenly Father's love for us caused him to send his son Jesus Christ into this world so that all these things can become things of the past (John 3:16-17). It doesn't matter how crude or disobedient we were; if and when we accept Jesus Christ as our savior, all these labels and lifestyles become history. They are no longer a part of us. 2 Cor. 5:17 states, "Therefore if any man be in Christ, he is a new creature: old things are passed away; behold, all things are become new." We are now washed and cleansed, with the Spirit of God dwelling within us. Now our old lifestyles can become a thing of the past.

Sometimes we believe what we have done was so bad that we hold onto the past even after becoming new, but let us all know that once you were set free by Jesus Christ, you are indeed free (John 8:36). No need to walk around feeling guilty and ashamed. Our sins are taken so far from us (Psalm 103:12) and have been forgotten by God (Micah 7:19); so, why should we walk around with its weight on our shoulders.

At times, the past is still present, but we must get to that place in our mind where we will never forget that our sins are forgiven, and if God forgives you, then you need to forgive yourself. Emancipate yourself from mental and sin slavery. Renew thoughts with scriptures. Let go of the guilt of the past and embrace his presence because He is present.

**YOUR PAST HAS PASSED; NOW, YOU HAVE THE PRESENCE OF THE HOLY SPIRIT AS A PRESENT.**

# Reflections:

1. Does the guilt of your past bound you?

_____

_____

_____

_____

_____

_____


2. What are some of the things that have been holding you back?

_____

_____

_____

_____

_____

_____

3. Has your past hinder you from progressing to your full capacity?

_____

_____

_____

_____

_____

_____

4. How is your past affecting your present/future?

_____

_____

_____

_____

_____

_____

# Day 8

## Snow White

---

*"And the LORD God commanded the man, saying, Of every tree of the garden thou mayest freely eat: but of the tree of the knowledge of good and evil, thou shalt not eat of it: for in the day that thou eatest thereof thou shalt surely die."*

*" For since by man came death, by man came also the resurrection of the dead. 22For as in Adam all die, even so in Christ shall all be made alive."*

*~Genesis 2:16-17*
*~1 Corinthians 15:21-22*

---

In the book of Genesis, God created. Everything was beautiful and sinless until!!!

Some people might be familiar with the fairytale of Snow White. It is a popular tale of a beautiful young girl who was a princess. Now, there was an evil queen, a witch, her stepmother, who had a magic mirror that declared Snow White the fairest in the land. The declaration from the magical mirror didn't sit well with the witch. She was determined to be the fairest but never got the satisfaction of her heart's desire. This disappointment brought about evil thoughts and plans by the evil queen, who put her plans into action by trying to get rid of her. Yet, she ended up in the hands of the seven dwarfs. The queen discovered she was still alive and disguised herself as a kind and friendly older woman. There she got the opportunity to introduce the vulnerable child to a poison apple, which Snow White did enjoy. She went into a long deep sleep similar to death. Fortunately, because it's a fairytale, a prince came one day, and in the end, she was given a kiss by this Prince, and she was back to a happily ever after life.

Is the Snow White story really a fairytale? Doesn't it sound familiar?

In the beginning (Genesis 1-2), God made everything, including mankind, and he made them beautiful. He was happy with his creation, and he saw everything good in his sight. Man (Adam) was placed to have dominion over all things on the earth. The man was given a companion (Eve), and all was going well until the jealous, evil, conniving serpent showed up (Genesis 3). Like the wicked witch, the serpent tricked this woman (Eve) into eating the forbidden fruit (God had already given specific instructions not to eat from that tree). She ate the fruit and presented it to the man who also ate the fruit. This act caused mankind to fall under the wrath of God, which led to death. It was actually the spiritual death of mankind.

So many evil spirits are roaming this earth, manipulating God's creatures into doing evil deeds. These spirits of jealousy, hatred, covetousness, strife, and much more are the ingredients that make this fruit of death that the enemy devises to take us out. If not careful, we will miss out on what our Father has in his kingdom for us.

However, a Prince called Jesus Christ came years after (Books of the Gospel). We were made alive because of his birth, life, death, burial, and resurrection (the kiss). We were redeemed and made to love again, all glory to the Almighty God. It is up to each of us if we get to live again as we have to accept the Prince and His kiss, then we will one day live happily ever after in Heaven with Him and all who receive Him.

# Reflections:

1. Do you understand how a person dies spiritually?

___

2. Are you a walking dead?

___

3. The Prince has come. Have you acknowledged and accepted Him? Have you received eternal life?

_____
_____
_____
_____
_____
_____
_____

# Day 9

# They Could Have, but They Couldn't...

*"Behold, this day thine eyes have seen how that the LORD had delivered thee to day into mine hand in the cave: and some bade me kill thee: but mine eye spared thee; and I said, I will not put forth mine hand against my lord; for he is the LORD's anointed."*

*~1 Samuel 24:10*

David was an anointed man of God, and so was King Saul, but because of jealousy, King Saul wanted to kill David. Because of this, they became enemies. Even though they were enemies, and David knew how much Saul intended to kill him, David remained respectful to him. 1 Samuel 24:10 and 1 Samuel 26 depict this fact. On two occasions, David could have gotten rid of his enemy. Still, the fact remains that despite Saul being unkind, he was God's anointed Servant.

There are people who, for some reason or another, would want to get rid of you however possible. They might have plotted, planned, and even come close to succeeding. However, as children of the Almighty God, it doesn't happen with ease. God has placed a mark upon His people; therefore, you can't be touched.

Job was tested and tried. His health was attacked, and he lost his family and all his possessions, but there was a limit to how far the enemy could go. God did allow satan to test Job, but satan was explicitly instructed not to kill him. He could have killed him, yes, but no. Yes, he had ways he could've but no, because God would not have allowed him to.

It's the same way our enemies might try to hurt, overcome and kill us, but God got us. There is a limit to how far the enemy can go. The Bible tells us in Isaiah 54:17 that no weapon formed against us shall prosper, so indeed, weapons may form, but they will not prevail against us.

Joseph's brothers wanted to kill Joseph (Genesis 37:18-28), so they plotted and began to put the plans into action, but they couldn't kill him for reasons and purpose. It wasn't their place to do so.

Pharaoh had the children of Israel backed up because the Red Sea was before them. They came in from behind, leaving nowhere for the Israelites to run. Still, God opened the sea right before their eyes and delivered them from the hands of their enemies (Exodus 14:13-28). The Egyptians could have, but they couldn't.

God has the final say in our lives, so our Omnipotent Father knows how to deliver us even if you get to a place where it seems you are cornered and the odds are against you.

## *Reflections:*

1. Can you remember at any point in your life where you know you could have died?

_____
_____
_____
_____
_____
_____

2. How fearful were you at that time?

_____
_____
_____
_____
_____
_____

3. Have you grown in faith, knowing that your life is in God's hand?

_____

_____

_____

_____

_____

_____


4. How did you get to that point where you gained such confidence?

_____

_____

_____

_____

_____

_____

# Day 10

# *The Separation is Preparation for Promotion*

*"Wherefore Come out from among them, and be ye separate, saith the Lord, And touch not the unclean thing; And I will receive you,"*

*~2 Corinthians 6:17*

A rotten fruit hung next to a wholesome other on a tree. They were both touching each other because of their closeness. Upon discovering the rotten fruit, the farmer decided to separate them from each other so the good fruit would not get contaminated. He threw out the rotten fruit and allowed the good fruit to remain on the vine, where it grew into fruition and was served well. If the bad fruit had stayed next to the good fruit, it would have caused that fruit to become rotten as well, and before you realize it, a whole bunch of fruits could get unfit for consumption.

Sometimes in life, we can be likened or compared to the fruits of that farmer's tree. We hang around and cling to others who may be bad influences. Some of our associates may be bad for our growth and purpose, some in detrimental ways. We have to be able to acknowledge if we are hanging in the wrong bunch and separate ourselves. Sometimes, we will recognize the fact but remain stubborn and keep hanging. Therefore God will cause things to happen so that we have no choice but to detach. The Bible tells us about being unequally yolked.

(2 Corinthians 6:14); poses the question, "Can two walk except they agree?" and advise us to separate ourselves (2 Corinthians 6:17) from

those people and things that can negatively influence us. We have to know if we are the bad fruit or the good fruit, but whatever fruit we are, we have to know our place.

Separation is necessary for us to grow. We need space and the right environment to allow our God-given purpose to manifest. This is also why Joseph in Genesis 37 had to be separated from his brothers to fulfill his purpose. Indeed it might be painful to separate depending on the closeness or the relationship of individuals, but it is not as painful as it would be in the end if that separation had not taken place. Sometimes we have to get away from a place because of its history or experiences that are in connection to that place. Too many bad experiences and memories might cause you to fear excelling. So it's a necessity that you separate from that area. In Genesis Chapter 12, Abraham was greatly rewarded after being instructed to separate himself from his home. At one point, he even had to choose separation from his own family. In Genesis Chapter 13, he saw the blessings of God in abundance; he became the father of many nations.

Do not be too attached to anything or anyone to cause you to be unable to separate yourself if needed. Your separation is preparation for your promotion

## *Reflections:*

1. Do you see yourself hanging with the wrong crowd? Can you attest?

_____
_____
_____
_____
_____
_____

2. What have you become so dependent on that it is difficult to sever those ties?

_____
_____
_____
_____
_____

3. Have you ever experienced a painful separation in your lifetime?

___

4. What results have your separation brought about? Was it worth it?

___

# Day 11

## *Don't Focus on the Process.*

## *Watch Out for the Product...*

*"My brethren, count it all joy when ye fall into divers temptations; knowing this, that the trying of your faith worketh patience. But let patience have her perfect work, that ye may be perfect and entire, wanting nothing."*

*~James 1:2-4*

Some of our experiences in life are very painful and heart-wrenching. They make you want just to give up and throw in the towel. Especially as believers, we go through some encounters that are enough for us to go crazy, but thanks be to God for grace and mercy. These experiences are not to kill us or bring us down but are molds that help shape us into what God destines us to become. The facts remain that it can be excruciating pain when you're being molded. Depending on your purpose, molds can come in different forms. You might go through sickness, abuse, rejection, and even betrayal. Some will experience multiple molds; this is how God refines us.

Luke 12:48 says, "to whom much is given, much is required." Some might say this scripture does not refer to God molding us; it means who God blesses abundantly should give abundantly. Yes, this may be true, but if we go deeper, we can analyze and come to the fact that if God had delivered you from all these sickness, rejection, hurt, and pain, then he is expecting you to use your powerful testimony to bring someone from despair to hope. He will use your situation for you to become a witness to his words and his promises.

Joseph was sold by his brothers, whom he loved, and Judas, one of his disciples, betrayed Jesus. He was mocked, talked about, and jeered, but we see what it was for. He endured all that for the salvation of his people. In all they encountered, neither Joseph nor Jesus watched, murmured, or complained; they went through their process, which gave them the character, demeanor, and strength to carry out what they were appointed to do by God.

God is our producer in this factory of life. He knows precisely what is needed to shape us into what He designed us to be. Therefore all we need to do is trust Him, trust the process and pray for the strength to endure. We focus too much on the process when the attention should be given to the product. Grapes get crushed to become wine, olives get pressed to become oil, and coconut gets chopped, crushed, and boiled to become oil. All rough and tough processes, but skip the process and pay attention to the products. How powerful they are.

As with the oils and the wine, the same with our lives, we might be crushed, broken, shaken, burned; you name it. The more purposeful you are, the more complex the process, but trust God and endure to the end.

**THE FINISH IS GREAT!**

# *Reflections:*

1. Ever asked the question, "God, why me? Why this? Recap that moment.

   _____
   _____
   _____
   _____
   _____
   _____

2. What are you presently experiencing that is so overwhelming?

   _____
   _____
   _____
   _____
   _____

3. Have you stopped to think about the future results?

_____
_____
_____
_____
_____
_____


4. How is your trust level in God when going through these processes?

_____
_____
_____
_____
_____
_____

# Day 12

# God's Puppet!
# He Alone Should Pull Our Strings.

*"No man can serve two masters: for either he will hate the one, and love the other; or else he will hold to the one, and despise the other. Ye cannot serve God and mammon."*

*~Matthew 6:24*

There is an old secular song I grew up hearing called "puppet on a string." The writer reassured his spouse that he was at her disposal, so like a puppet on a string, she could go ahead and pull him however she desired, and he would move in obedience. He was making sure she knew how much he loved her, and it was so much that he was willing to please her totally.

Puppets are dependent on their master, so there is nothing they can do without that puppet master. The master has to pull his strings for him to move. We are like human puppets who all have a master, but who is your master? The Bible tells us that we should be obedient to one master and that master should be He who created us. If we are not obedient to Him, we have a different master. Matthew 6:24 says, "No man can serve two masters: for either he will hate the one, and love the other; or else he will hold to the one, and despise the other. Ye cannot serve God and mammon." It's a simple saying that if we are living double lifestyles, we are being obedient to two masters. Still, it cannot work because one master will be loved or respected more than the other.

Only God knows His plan for us, and His plans are good for us (Jeremiah 29:11). Any other plans are deceitful and harmful to us. Therefore if we are puppets on strings, we are God's puppets and should only be pulled by Him. He alone should get our full, undivided attention. He should get our obedience because if we say we belong to Him but obey Him not, we are liars. The one we obey is our master, and he is pulling the strings. So today, let's ask ourselves, "Am I God's puppet? Who's really pulling my strings?"

Romans 8:14
"For as many as are led by the Spirit of God, they are the sons of God."

# *Reflections:*

1. Take a moment and consider, who's really pulling your strings?

   _____

   _____

   _____

   _____

   _____

   _____


2. Who are you most obedient to?

   _____

   _____

   _____

   _____

   _____

   _____

3. Are you switching masters conditionally?

4. Are you willing to stay faithful to one?

# Day 13

# Name Brand / Brand Name

---

*"be it known unto you all, and to all the people of Israel, that by the name of Jesus Christ of Nazareth, whom ye crucified, whom God raised from the dead, even by him doth this man stand here before you whole. This is the stone which was set at nought of you builders, which is become the head of the corner. Neither is there salvation in any other: for there is none other name under heaven given among men, whereby we must be saved."*

*~Acts 4:10-12*

---

The name you represent says a lot about you. What is your logo, and what Brand are you wearing?

When it comes to shopping, whether for clothes, food, shoes, a house, a car, or whatever the need be, specific names stand out and tend to carry more weight in expense. Some people would love to be able to own these Brand items, but unfortunately, they cannot afford to. It's sad knowing that because of your class in society, you may be deprived of the opportunity to own certain goods and services of quality.

However, there is one name that you can proudly wear no matter your race, color, or creed. It is available to all mankind, whether rich, poor, or middle standard. It is the biggest, most expensive name one could carry, but it comes to us for free. It is the name above all names, the name at which every knee should bow (Philippians 2:9-11). It is the only name through which all men can be saved - The name of Jesus Christ. All we have to do is believe and receive him as our savior (John 1:12).

It's a privilege to know that we wear the name of Christ. It means we are royalty, Prince, and Princesses (1 Peter 2:9). It matters not who our earthly families are or their class in society; once you're adopted into the kingdom of God, your name changes. Our name also gives us power over the forces of darkness; it gives us access to our Father in heaven anytime. 2 Chronicles 7:14 tells us of our benefits when we carry His name. The name of Jesus is the only name that stands forever. This name is always valid when all other Brands may expire or get outdated. It stands uncontested.

In the world games, each country's representatives proudly wear their colors and flags to show who they represent. This act of representation is the same attitude that we should portray when we wear the name of Christ. Daniel and the three Hebrew boys are perfect examples of how we should be. They knew they were in Babylon but still wore their God's name, even facing adversities. Let's stand boldly and wear our Brand proudly. It is the best Brand you could wear.

Are you wearing His name? If not, start doing so now; it will be worth the price.

**FREE**

# *Reflections:*

1. What is the most expensive Brand that you have ever owned?

_____

_____

_____

_____

_____

_____

2. Did you work or save to possess such a name?

_____

_____

_____

_____

_____

_____

3. How much assistance can this particular Brand name give?

_____

_____

_____

_____

_____

_____


4. What prevents you from wearing this most expensive yet priceless name?

_____

_____

_____

_____

_____

# Day 14

# Just One Stone

*"And David put his hand in his bag, and took thence a stone, and slang it, and smote the Philistine in his forehead, that the stone sunk into his forehead; and he fell upon his face to the earth."*

*~1 Samuel 17:49*

The story of how David conquered Goliath with just a sling and a stone after the Philippines came up against the children of Israel is a well-known story in the Bible (1 Samuel 17). Goliath, because of his stature, was considered a giant. His height, when calculated, was equal to 9 feet 9 inches in today's terms. It was also a fact that Goliath was an undefeated soldier everyone feared, so when David, who was opposite in stature, stood up to him, he thought it a mockery. He laughed at little David and ridiculed him because he was confident he'd already won. On the other hand, David was no soldier but just a shepherd boy who spent his time tending to sheep. He was skillful in caring for his sheep and warding off animals but never fought in a war. Confidence in his skills didn't frighten him one bit; he was confident in the God he served. God had given him victory over fierce animals before, so he knew the power of his God. He knew God was and still is a deliverer. There was no fear in him because he knew 2 Timothy 1:17. So when he faced this giant, all he had was his stones and a sling; indeed, with the strike of one stone, the giant was down. It took just one stone.

Like David, some giants face us at times and want to challenge us, but unlike David, we often get overcome by fear. We panic and forget who our God is, so the giants take us down before we know it. Today we are being encouraged and reminded that all it takes is one stone. It might seem small but do know that little is much when God is in it. Remember our Day One Devotional about the small axe, which is just reassurance that once God is with us, we can take giants down because it's not us but the God in us (1 John 4:4). Our stones might be in different shapes; some might be in the shape of prayer, some may be in the shape of fasting, and some as the Word of God, which may be praise and worship. Still, whatever is your best stone, with God, it is powerful. Don't be overcome by your giants; stand in boldness, shoot that stone, and watch your Goliath fall.

> One stone is all it takes.
> You need just that one stone.

# *Reflections:*

1. From reading this text, can you name your most powerful stone?

___

___

___

___

___

2. How often do you use your stone to conquer your fears?

___

___

___

___

___

3. What is hindering you from using that stone?

_____

_____

_____

_____

_____

_____


4. Has your stone been so long laid aside that it is no longer easily accessible?

_____

_____

_____

_____

_____

_____

# Day 15

## A Spiritual MRI

*"But the LORD said unto Samuel, Look not on his countenance, or on the height of his stature; because I have refused him: for the LORD seeth not as man seeth; for man looketh on the outward appearance, but the LORD looketh on the heart."*

~1 Samuel 16:7

A mirror shows our outside image, so we can see what we look like on the outward. We know what is evident to the naked eyes. However, an MRI (Magnetic

Resonance Imaging) is used to see deeper than the outward. It detects illnesses such as growths and tumors that develop internally. These are impossible to view from the outside; therefore, an MRI might be required.

The human eyes are similar to the mirror, while the eyes of God are similar to the MRI. There is only a limit to what someone can see when looking at you through the natural eyes. They only see what the physical eyes can, and that's what's on the outside. They see the displayed behavior and so often judge because of it. This display is often just a show, with your true identity or characteristics hidden beneath. However, a person's outward appearance cannot deceive God. 1 Samuel 16:7 states, "But the LORD said unto Samuel, Look not on his countenance, or on the height of his stature; because I have refused him: for *the LORD seeth* not as man seeth; for man looketh on the outward appearance, but the LORD looketh on the heart."

God knows our hearts; He knows our minds, and He knows our thoughts. We need not worry about what men think about us because it's how God sees us that matters. Men sometimes judge us because of how we appear in their eyes, but if they were to see our hearts, it would paint a totally different picture of us. Even our abilities are questionable based on our looks which is sometimes misleading.

If our God, who is the Omniscient God (He knows all things), should scan us, what would he find hidden on the inside. How is our inner man (the spirit)? Are we filled with tumors of hatred, growth of maliciousness, sicknesses of unforgiveness, and diseases of all kinds of sins? God forbid. We may be tainted, and some may be the results of our past. But, even still, our Heavenly Father is a doctor of all doctors for our natural illnesses and the spiritual. If we allow Him, He can perform that surgery to take away these things (Isaiah 53:5). Open your heart and let Him in; permit Him to operate in you and on you today. He can do all things (Ephesians 3:20).

# *Reflections:*

1. What is your mirror reflecting?

   _____

   _____

   _____

   _____

   _____

   _____

2. Is your mirror image the same as your MRI?

   _____

   _____

   _____

   _____

   _____

   _____

3. Is there surgery required for your Spirit Man?

___

4. What brought you to the place of spiritual diseases?

___

# Day 16

# *Unction to Function*

*"The Spirit of the Lord GOD is upon me; because the LORD hath anointed me to preach good tidings unto the meek; he hath sent me to bind up the brokenhearted, to proclaim liberty to the captives, and the opening of the prison to them that are bound; to proclaim the acceptable year of the LORD, and the day of vengeance of our God; to comfort all that mourn; to appoint unto them that mourn in Zion, to give unto them beauty for ashes, the oil of joy for mourning, the garment of praise for the spirit of heaviness; that they might be called trees of righteousness, the planting of the LORD, that he might be glorified."*

*~Isaiah 61:1-3*

# The word unction means to anoint or treat with oil.

In motor vehicles, the use of engine oil is essential. It lubricates the moving metal pieces inside the engine of the vehicle to ensure they move freely. This operation gives a longer life to the engine and fewer breakdowns. We can put it this way; the vehicle needs its unction to function effectively.

Christians, like the vehicles, need their oil (the anointing) to function effectively and effortlessly. Without this unction, the works of Jesus cannot be demonstrated through us. Jesus said to his disciples (John 14:12) he that believes on me, the works that I do shall he do also and greater". In the book of Acts, when he was ready to ascend into heaven, he told them (Acts 1:8) "but ye shall receive power, after that the HOLY GHOST is come upon you: and ye shall be witnesses unto me both in Jerusalem, and in all Judaea, and in Samaria, and unto the uttermost part of the earth." They obeyed and went into the upper room for ten days, and the prophecy was fulfilled on the day of Pentecost (Acts 2). After this, the disciples performed miracles, signs, and wonders powerfully. Not only that but also sharing and caring among brethren, so no one had lacked. All this was an example of unction to function. The HOLY GHOST gave the unction, and then they were able to operate effectively in the community.

We need this same unction in today's world. Christians need the anointing of the Holy Spirit to operate effortlessly and effectively (Luke 10:19). We also will be able to have a longer and stronger spiritual life with fewer breakdowns.

There is a need, people are dying, but we do not possess that power needed to carry out the assignment that God has placed on us. We have to make ourselves available and give ourselves time to tarry in the presence of God. We need to fast, pray and apply the word to receive our unction. Jesus himself received unction to function (Isaiah 61); therefore, it is required.

Like the vehicles, let's pull into our HOLY GHOST garage to fill our oils.

# STRIVE FOR THE UNCTION TO FUNCTION.

# Reflections:

1. How desirous are you of functioning in Christ?

   _____

   _____

   _____

   _____

   _____

   _____

2. Are you willing to sacrifice that time and effort to receive the unction?

   _____

   _____

   _____

   _____

3. What are some of the works that you would love to see demonstrated in your life?

_____

_____

_____

_____

_____

_____

_____

# Day 17

# Pleasing Everybody

*"For do I now persuade men, or God? or do I seek to please men? for if I yet pleased men, I should not be the servant of Christ."*

~Galatians 1:10

There is a story about a father and son on their way to the market with their donkey. While walking alongside the donkey, someone approached them, suggesting that the young son should ride the donkey while his father walked. He obeyed, only to be approached by another person who suggested that the father should be the one who rides the donkey and have the son walking, which he obeyed. On several occasions, they were approached with different suggestions, which they gave ear to each time they were approached. In all this confusion, the man and his son were ridiculed, criticized, mocked, and cursed out because, at one point, they both ended up carrying the donkey, which was out of the ordinary. Eventually, he realized that he was trying to please everybody, and it was impossible to do so.

In life, you might think it's cool to be loved by all, so to reach this goal, you will attempt to do things to please everyone around you. In reality, we cannot; it is impossible to please everyone, so we aim to please God. Know what God expects from us by reading the word and applying it to our lives. Pleasing everyone brings about confusion, hurt, and pain.

The devil tempted Jesus in Matthew 4: 1-11, but Jesus resisted and did what was right. The crowd often told him to do things that would please their ego, but he held his composure. Jesus already knew who He was, and so His intentions were never to please anyone. He came to do his father's will, which is precisely what He did. They threw words challenging Him that if He was the son of God, He should prove it to them, but He did not surrender to the voice of men at no time.

Like Jesus, we will be tempted, tried, and advised to do things according to others' opinions. Some may seem reasonable; some may seem wise; some might not even make sense, but whatever advice or instructions we follow, we have to ensure it is in line with the will of God and not contrary to His teachings. We must remember that there is a way that seems right unto man, but the end thereof is the ways of death (Proverbs 14:12).

Don't be likened to that man who tried pleasing everybody; you can end up satisfying the devil himself and be left behind. Be like Jesus who said, I came to do the will of my father (John 6:38). So let our aim and our priority be to please God and not man. Men are full of opinions, but truth and facts are of God.

# *Reflections:*

1. Have you ever been bombarded with suggestions that you end up confused about instead of clarified?

   _____

   _____

   _____

   _____

   _____

   _____

2. Who do you listen to for directions in daily endeavors?

   _____

   _____

   _____

   _____

   _____

   _____

3. Do you know God's voice?

_____
_____
_____
_____
_____
_____
_____

#  18

# The Boy Who Cried Wolf/Sounding the Trumpet

*"And this gospel of the kingdom shall be preached in all the world for a witness unto all nations; and then shall the end come."*

*~Matthew 24:14*

From as early as I can remember, I have heard about the Lord's coming. These words have been sounding for decades and will continue to sound off until He appears. We can see numerous times where "Repent for the Kingdom of God is at hand" has been repeatedly preached. John the Baptist preached it, Jesus preached it; it was preached in the Old Testament, yet we are still here preaching the same message. It is a continuous alarm throughout the world. People have taken this warning seriously over the years, and some have died; still, they haven't witnessed this coming. After living a righteous life, some believers have given up and turned back to their sinful lifestyle because they have not seen the manifestation of this continuous alarm of Jesus' return.

Now, there is a story of a boy who cried wolf. He was a shepherd boy who enjoyed making false alarms about wolves coming to attack his sheep. People would always leave their busy schedules to come to his aid. Only to discover that he was, as always, making false alarms. He was just telling lies to get attention. But it so happened that, one day, when he least expected, he was tending to his flock, and wolves actually came. This time, he cried and cried and cried, but no one came to assist him. He realized no one showed up because they thought this was just another false alarm.

In today's world, the cry of Evangelists repeatedly sounds off, just like the boy who cried "wolf." The difference between the shepherd boy and those who are spreading the gospel is that the shepherd boy was prophesying without realizing that it would come to pass, while Evangelists and believers of the Gospel are prophesying that which is true and they know will come to pass.

People will ignore a real cry. If they do this, they will also deny the real alarm of our savior's return, just because it's being repeated, and it seems nothing has happened. Rest assured, there will be a coming of the Lord Jesus. It's going to be a sudden appearance. The word tells us that He shall come like a thief in the night (Revelation 16:15, Matthew 24:43, 1 Thessalonians 5:2), and no man knows the day or the hour, not even the angels in heaven (Matthew 24:36).

The cry of the Lord's return may sound like that of the boy who cried wolf, but let's use it as an example that we always have to be prepared because, indeed, on a day when least expected, the Lord will show up. Don't criticize those who are sounding the alarm. Be on the alert because the son of God will appear any minute. Now is not the time to give up; it's time to be more alert.

# *Reflections:*

1. Have you ever really questioned Christ's return?

   _____

   _____

   _____

   _____

   _____

2. Is he coming again, or is it a myth?

   _____

   _____

   _____

   _____

   _____

3. How prepared are you for His coming if and when He comes again?

_____

_____

_____

_____

_____

_____


4. Do you sound the alarm of His coming?

_____

_____

_____

_____

_____

_____

# Day 19

# *Planted Not Buried*

> *"But as for you, ye thought evil against me; but God meant it unto good, to bring to pass, as it is this day, to save much people alive."*
>
> *~Genesis 50:20*

Taking a seed and putting it under the earth so that it can grow is called planting. Taking something and putting or hiding it underground is also called burying. Even though planting and burying are somewhat similar in actions, the difference in outcome is tremendous.

When something is being planted, it grows roots that take hold of the soil, and then a small plant will begin to emerge through the earth with care. Along with the sunshine and rain, it will grow into a massive tree that hopefully brings fruit. The buried thing, however, will decompose and rot. It is then good for nothing.

Sometimes in life, we go through some stages where we feel like we are being buried under the earth. We might go through these phases based on how someone dealt with us; maybe we've been abused, mistreated, beaten, spoken down to, or disrespected, just to name a few, and we are left feeling just as dead. We feel like we are left under the earth to rot, but this is an opportunity for us to take root. Find the fertile soil and become attached, then you will notice that instead of dying, you will be like that tree planted by the rivers of water (Psalm 1). You shall spring forth and grow strong then become the branches attached to the vine (John 15: 1-5).

It's time to rise. You've been thrown out and placed under the dirt, but know that you have been planted and not buried. The enemy should have killed you before burying you. Still, you were buried alive; this is why you were planted instead of buried. Don't choke yourself to death with tears, for then you'll be helping to take yourself out. Instead, water yourself with the word and allow the Son (Jesus) to shine on you and grow into that beautiful and fruitful tree you were truly meant to be. Then you will begin to feel and see your worth as your fruits begin to grow, seeds begin to spread, and you will become a great forest.

# *Reflections:*

1. At your lowest point, do you consider yourself planted or buried?

_____

_____

_____

_____

_____

2. What are some situations that bring you to that place of feeling buried?

_____

_____

_____

_____

_____

_____

3. How do you overcome that low season in your life?

_____

_____

_____

_____

_____

_____


4. As of today, can you see yourself planted and not buried?

_____

_____

_____

_____

_____

_____

# Day 20

# Adorn/ Enhance Self

*"I beseech you therefore, brethren, by the mercies of God, that ye present your bodies a living sacrifice, holy, acceptable unto God, which is your reasonable service. And be not conformed to this world: but be ye transformed by the renewing of your mind, that ye may prove what is that good, and acceptable, and perfect, will of God."*

*~Romans 12:1-2*

We live in an era where a particular figure or image is painted as beauty. Suppose someone is not the perfect shape, size, or appearance as painted by the media. In that case, they're considered ugly or out of shape and unattractive. People get bullied, especially in schools, for being different. They experience name-calling and constant belittling, leading many of them into depression and, worst-case scenario, suicidal thoughts. But what is the meaning of real beauty? How is someone classified as attractive? Is it the makeup, the clothes, the shape, or the figure?

The truth is, these are not the actual definition of beauty. Beauty lies within. The Bible teaches us that it's not the outward look that's important but your ways. Your character and behavior, the inner man (your Spirit), speak volumes. Even specific scriptures (1Timothy 2:9 and 1 Peter 3:3) specify to women about being godly and doing good works as a means of adorning instead of enhancing with vain things. These passages encourage the adorning of our ways and behavior as tools in attracting others to our God and us. When we have beauty within, it shines on the outside and needs no effort to win others' attention. One can be outwardly attractive, but their character will push others away from them.

Our godly ways make us beautiful, keep people attracted to us, and always want to be around us. Being beautiful in your mannerism can land you favor among men. Daniel had an excellent spirit (Daniel 1), and it caused him to receive favor amongst the Babylonians.

Having physical beauty is wonderful, but it's all vanity. Let's invest in spiritual surgeries, cut off bad habits, destructive behaviors, unkindness, greed, and selfishness, and add love, peace, meekness, and kindness to our hearts. Let's exercise the spiritual as much as we exercise the natural. Work on truth, mercy, and compassion, and this world will be the most beautiful world we've ever seen. It pays to be beautiful, but the real beauty comes from within.

# *Reflections:*

1. How would you rate your appearance as an individual?

_____
_____
_____
_____
_____
_____

2. Would God see you as the same beautiful person you appear to be in the natural?

_____
_____
_____
_____
_____
_____

3. Identify some attitudes that you possess that you know are not so beautiful?

_____
_____
_____
_____
_____
_____

4. Identify the attitudes that you possess which make you beautiful?

_____
_____
_____
_____
_____
_____

5. Compare and make the necessary adjustments. Seek God's help.

# Day 21

# Strange Addictions

*"Blessed is the man that walketh not in the counsel of the ungodly, nor standeth in the way of sinners, Nor sitteth in the seat of the scornful. But his delight is in the law of the LORD; And in his law doth he meditate day and night."*

*"This book of the law shall not depart out of thy mouth; but thou shalt meditate therein day and night, that thou mayest observe to do according to all that is written therein: for then thou shalt make thy way prosperous, and then thou shalt have good success."*

~Psalm 1:1-2
~Joshua 1:8

What is an addiction? An addiction is a dependency or a condition of being addicted to a particular substance, thing, or activity. It might be a craving or a habit that have you fixed on a specific thing.

There are some strange addictions that I have come across, and I have had a few. Addictions are no joke depending on what one is addicted to. They can be harmful, but are they all? As stated previously, I've had a few addictions of my own. There was a time when I was addicted to eating things like ashes, chalk, charcoal, and baby powder. Whattt? Yes, I was there, so I know too well what it is like to be addicted. It's that craving where it feels as if not satisfied, you would go crazy. You have to get that thing, and the minute you get it, wow! There's this satisfying feeling.

However, these addictions can harm one's health and well-being. Some folks are addicted to drugs, alcohol, cleaning, eating, etc. These are more common addictions but still can have adverse effects.

There is a program that I've seen on TV. that looks into the lives of people with strange addictions. They classify them as odd because of the things people get addicted to that are hardly ever heard of. People are addicted to eating glass, plastic bags, dirty diapers, and drinking blood, to name a few. If I didn't see it, I wouldn't believe it myself, but it's real, and as someone who can relate to strange addictions, I totally understand how it feels. It gives satisfaction. However, many of these addictions come about because of deficiencies or ease of emotional distress, but something drove them there.

So, where is this going? Is there an addiction that is actually beneficial? Just think, wouldn't it be great if our strange addiction comes about because of hunger for God. So we would get addicted to the Bible, praying, fasting, and worshipping? This type of addiction would be one of the best strange addictions one could develop as it would satisfy our Spirit. It would bring healing and help us change our ways (Psalm 119:9). If we delight in the word of God and get addicted to this, we will flourish (Psalm 1:2-3). There are scriptures for every situation.

Suppose we could just get into the habit of drawing for the Bible when we feel depressed, singing a song of worship when we feel sad, and praying when we get anxious. In that case, we will have a "strange" addiction, but one that will eliminate adverse effects and bring positive changes.

### Let's Get Addicted!

# *Reflections:*

1. Have you experienced any addictions in your lifetime?

_____

_____

_____

_____

_____


2. In what way did they affect your life?

_____

_____

_____

_____

_____

3. How did you overcome them, or is there still a struggle?

_____

_____

_____

_____

_____

_____


4. Want to try a new habit (reading the Word of God)?

_____

_____

_____

_____

_____

_____

# Day 22

# A Broken Pencil

*"And the vessel that he made of clay was marred in the hand of the potter: so he made it again another vessel, as seemed good to the potter to make it. Then the word of the LORD came to me, saying, O house of Israel, cannot I do with you as this potter? saith the LORD. Behold, as the clay is in the potter's hand, so are ye in mine hand, O house of Israel."*

*~Jeremiah 18:4-6*

I was dosing off into sleep when God began showing me a pencil. I wondered what this pencil was for then he made me understand that we are like pencils in a writer's hand. However, we have a choice of what is written about us, so our lives are the stories we write in this book called the society or the world. We must ensure that whatever we write is positive in enhancing the lives of others and deserving of a reward from God. Indeed, our scripts will be rewarded. (Rev.22:12).

However, this was not the only point He was showing me. The pencil broke, and He made me understand that even though it was broken, it was still usable. It didn't lose its purpose. It didn't stop writing because it was broken. We sometimes might get broken in life, we might get hurt, but it doesn't mean that we are no longer valuable. We might be on a little pause, but It doesn't mean that we are no longer of use. Indeed some might want to throw us away if and when we get broken but not God. When our point breaks, we get resharpened by his word. His love keeps us and gives us the chance to go on. God can hold us and continue using us to make great recordings.

There is an eraser also (the blood of Jesus) that we own that leaves no trace whenever we make mistakes. It blots out every error, and then we can proceed with writing our story. Jeremiah 18 describes us as clay in the potter's hand, so we can also consider ourselves pencils in the writer's hand.

Do you feel broken? Don't be discouraged; the writer is ready to resharpen you. If not sharpened, the pencil has no effect. The pencil must go into the sharpener and be shaved down to the lead to be used again. It may be a painful process to get resharpened, but you become great once that process is over. You can write stories that will impact lives. Your story can change the world.

Until your very end point,
be the best pencil that writes the best stories.

# *Reflections:*

1. What stories are you writing in life's book?

___

___

___

___

___

___

2. Are they affecting lives in positive ways?

___

___

___

___

___

___

3. Have you ever been broken and thought you were no longer useful?

_____

_____

_____

_____

_____

_____


4. Are you prepared and ready to be resharpened and re-used?

_____

_____

_____

_____

_____

_____

# Day 23

# What Are Your Thoughts?

---

*"Finally, brethren, whatsoever things are true, whatsoever things are honest, whatsoever things are just, whatsoever things are pure, whatsoever things are lovely, whatsoever things are of good report; if there be any virtue, and if there be any praise, think on these things."*

*~Philippians 4:8*

---

Some things are easier said than done, especially when on the outside looking in. Someone will say, "If you were in my shoe, or you know my name but not my story."

They are referring to others' reactions to them when they disapprove of their behavior towards a situation. One doesn't understand the trauma another person has been through because people's tolerance levels are not the same. Hence we find that situations affect individuals differently. Some experiences have people scarred for life. The first thing they remember when they awake and the last thing before going to bed is that incident or accident that affected them negatively. These experiences are enough to drive one into a bad mood and attitude. The more we think about these bad experiences, the more they affect us negatively.

The mind is one of the most powerful assets that a human being possesses. How we face the different life cycles is influenced by what goes on in our minds. I believe this is one of the reasons Paul in Romans 12:2 says that our minds must be renewed to please God. The mind must be transformed (retrained) to positive thinking for one to live a positive, God-pleasing life.

There is a word called faith, defined as believing in what we can't see, including Christ (Hebrews 11:6). To do such, we have to allow our minds to cancel anything contrary to such. Getting over trauma can be difficult as memories tend to linger, leaving us believing that these memories will never go away.

Even the occurrences of today's world are leaving our minds in fear and worry. Still, this text today will remind us of Philippians 4:8 "Finally, brethren, whatsoever things are true, whatsoever things are honest, whatsoever things are just, whatsoever things are pure, whatsoever things are lovely, whatsoever things are of good report; if there be any virtue, and if there be any praise, think on these things."

# *Reflections:*

1. What thoughts occupy your mind the most?

_____

_____

_____

_____

_____

2. Are these thoughts motivating or destructive?

_____

_____

_____

_____

_____

3. How much does your history contribute to these thoughts?

___

___

___

___

___

___

___

4. Have you tried renewing your thoughts?

___

___

___

___

___

___

5. Do you think changing the mindset will help to heal those past wounds?

___
___
___
___
___
___
___

# Day 24

# Jealousy, A Big Killer

*"And Cain talked with Abel his brother: and it came to pass, when they were in the field, that Cain rose up against Abel his brother, and slew him. And the LORD said unto Cain, Where is Abel thy brother? And he said, I know not: Am I my brother's keeper? And he said, What hast thou done? the voice of thy brother's blood crieth unto me from the ground."*

*~Genesis 4:8-10*

The first physical death mentioned in the Bible results from murder caused by jealousy. It's written in Chapter 4 of the book of Genesis, where two brothers lived and had unique individual skills. God required them both to offer sacrifices unto him. It's further stated that they both obeyed the request, but God accepted one sacrifice above the other. This decision by God; stirred up the jealousy within, which led to the first act of murder being committed.

Truth be told, we have found ourselves on either end of the fence at some point in our lives. There are times when we may have become jealous of someone or something, and there are times when we were the ones envied. It's not a good thing to fall on either side. Jealousy can lead to someone hating or being hated, lying or being lied to, committing acts of murder, or being murdered, as was demonstrated by the scriptures. Basically, jealousy will (if not rooted out from the seed) spring up into a tree of bitterness. It can lead to covetousness which is a sin.

Jealousy is a means of distraction (Day 6 Devotional) that should be avoided at all costs, as we may overlook our own qualities and potentials by focusing on others' assets. It is not of God and will lead us into temptations. People are ignored and overlooked because of jealousy. Some people are driven to fear showing their true potential because of jealousy hanging around them. Once discerned, it is good to separate ourselves from these negative energies (Day 10 Devotional). Jealousy, however, can affect someone positively as they desire to become as successful as another. This feeling doesn't come with anyone getting hurt or hated, but with admiration.

In Luke 15:11-32, there's also a demonstration of two brothers who grew up, and one went his way living lavishly while the other remained humble at home. In the end, the brother who went his way returned broke and filthy. The father was so happy about his son's return that he called for a celebration instantly. The son who remained home and faithful to dad was upset because jealousy crept in. He saw it as a sign of preference even though he was the devoted son.

Some of us may relate to this text, but if we look at the real reason behind the father's celebration, we know he was just grateful for his son's return. Let us stop to think before getting jealous and acting upon our feelings. Solomon 8:6 tells us that jealousy is as cruel as the grave. If we know what a grave is, we'll see that jealousy is ruinous. It's a killer.

# *Reflections:*

1. Have you ever been jealous of anyone/in what way were you jealous?

   _____

   _____

   _____

   _____

   _____

   _____

2. Do you still possess a spirit of jealousy?

   _____

   _____

   _____

   _____

   _____

   _____

3. Has anyone ever been jealous of you in a way that affected you negatively?

___

___

___

___

___

___

4. Do you know you can be jealous but in a way that will boost you to improve yourself?

___

___

___

___

___

___

# Day 25

# You Are Light!

*"Ye are the light of the world. A city that is set on an hill cannot be hid. Neither do men light a candle, and put it under a bushel, but on a candlestick; and it giveth light unto all that are in the house. Let your light so shine before men, that they may see your good works, and glorify your Father which is in heaven."*

*~Matthew 5:14-16*

In the beginning, the earth was dark (Genesis 1), but God came and called light into darkness. What a beauty that must have been. Imagine being in a dark room, and then someone turns the light on, and everything around you becomes clear and visible. It even gives off a more relaxed feeling knowing you can see all around you.

Well, we as humans are compared to that darkness when we have a life without Christ, but when we accept him as our Lord, we become that light that brightens the world. As we become children of God, we have a responsibility to bring light to those still in darkness. Those who are in despair, we are their light of hope; those who are sick should find a light of healing in us, and those who hunger should look to us as a light for feeding, a light of shelter to those who are shelterless. We can't be called light if we are not shining. If we are called light, and no one can see their way through us, it means we either have gone dim or are blown out.

Is it that you are a rechargeable light and therefore need charging, or are you like a lamp that occasionally needs oil, and your oil has run out?

People depend on us to shine our light so they can escape the darkness. There is nothing like a selfish light; therefore, we can't be selfish. Once a light begins to shine, it lights up all around unless a shade has been placed over it to confine it to a limited area. God has not restricted us, so we are allowed to shine all around. If you find yourself confined, the enemy has crept in and put a shade over you to keep you limited. But, you have the power to overcome the enemy who is himself darkness; you have the power to outshine him when he attacks. You are more than conquerors (Romans 8:37).

Let's get our lights shining brightly, so we can go out into the world. We need the oil of prayer, the recharging of the Spirit by plugging into the word of God, re-igniting our flames with fastings, and not forgetting the assembling of the saints coming together in love(Hebrews 10:24-25). These acts will allow us to be a significant glare of lights shining throughout the world.

# *Reflections:*

1. Do you see yourself as light, and why?

   _____

   _____

   _____

   _____

   _____

   _____

2. How far is your light shining?

   _____

   _____

   _____

   _____

   _____

   _____

3. What are some effects you have made in shining your light on others?

_____

_____

_____

_____

_____

_____

4. Is there a shade blocking the spread of your light?

_____

_____

_____

_____

_____

_____

# Day 26

## Seed Sowers

*"Be not deceived; God is not mocked: for whatsoever a man soweth, that shall he also reap."*

*~Galatians 6:7*

I can't help reverting to the sayings of my Jamaican culture. Some phrases we use are unheard of but make clear sense. I learned from some of these and still can refer to them from time to time.

We often use a compelling and factual statement: "you caan plant cawn an a peas yuh waan reap." This statement means you can't be planting seeds of corn with the expectation of reaping peas. Factually if you want a harvest of peas, then it's obvious you'll have to plant peas grains. Whatever the seeds are, they will be precisely what's harvested. Therefore, if you plant hot peppers, don't expect a tree full of cherries to harvest. And another thing to remember is when one seed is planted, it springs forth, and its tree will produce much fruit.

As we live among each other on this earth, we must interact with others and communicate daily. Whether you are in school, on the job, in church, or in whatever group we associate with, even in our homes, we are expected to treat each other with kindness and love (1 Corinthians 13). However, some of us overlook that expectation, and we treat others less. There is no compassion, mercy, love, or humility towards some persons, especially if they seem to be of a lower standard. God, however, warned us against such behaviors and is described as respecting a person (James 2:1-9).

Let's be aware that our actions towards others are like planting seeds. How we treat our fellow humans is an investment in our future well-being (Proverbs 28:27). However, if we treat others, whether mean and degrading or kind and loving, the same shall be our reward (Matthew 5:5-7, Luke 6:38). It, therefore, behooves us to do good for good to come at us. It will be a ricochet of your behavior towards another. Therefore let us check the seeds we are planting among friends, families, associates, our sisters and brothers, and even our children. Some people will plant seeds according to what has been planted in them, so we must be mindful that we overcome by renewing our minds (Day 23 Devotional). If you have realized that you have already planted seeds you do not want to reap, dig up, chop out and start over.

# *Reflections:*

1. Think about the seeds you planted. Are you excitedly waiting for harvest?

_____

_____

_____

_____

_____

2. Were you used as soil for someone else's bad seeds?

_____

_____

_____

_____

_____

3. How was Christ in your life affected your planting?

___

4. Are there seeds already planted that need to be destroyed?

___

# Day 27

## Stone Throwers

*"And they which heard it, being convicted by their own conscience, went out one by one, beginning at the eldest, even unto the last: and Jesus was left alone, and the woman standing in the midst. When Jesus had lifted up himself, and saw none but the woman, he said unto her, Woman, where are those thine accusers? hath no man condemned thee? She said, No man, Lord. And Jesus said unto her, Neither do I condemn thee: go, and sin no more."*

~John 8:9-11

## "If you live in a glass house, don't throw stones!"

There are times in our lives when we have messed up and fallen short of God's glory. I surely can raise my hand to say I've been guilty on numerous occasions of things that, if it had not been for the grace of God, I know I wouldn't be around till now. Thanks be to God for his mercy and grace.

In John, Chapter 8, verses 1 to 11 illustrate a woman caught in an adulterous act (unfaithful to her spouse). This act came with a penalty where the guilty party was stoned to death. Oh, how I thank God for Jesus because if it were in these times, I, for one, would have been stoned.

Jesus, the son of God, was approached by accusers who were ready to stone this woman to death, but because of a heart of mercy, he had compassion for her. He also knew that the people who accused this woman were all hypocrites as they had issues and behaviors that would have achieved the same punishment. Jesus stooped and wrote on the ground, then charged them, saying, "the one without sin, let him be the one to cast the first stone." At that point, not one of these people could lift their hands because they were all sinners. We can hide from a man but never from God.

In our society, in this day and age, there are constant replays of this incident only with a different ending. Jesus, not physically present, has forgiven us, but men still throw stones, not remembering their faults. Some are quick to throw a stone without giving persons a chance to redeem themselves. Stones get thrown from different angles without persons checking themselves (Matthew 7:5). We all need to know that we all have sinned and come short of God's glory (Romans 3:23), and unless we all repent, we shall likewise perish (Luke 13:2-5). It matters not what we do, be it murder, lie, steal, covet, malice, fornicate, etc., we are all as guilty as each other if we don't repent. No one can say they have never sinned (1 John 1:8-10).

We don't know what brought a person to commit whatever act they committed, but let us be merciful and correct in love and meekness; we too shall fall (Galatians 6:1).

> Don't be quick to throw stones;
> a stone might come back at you.

# Reflections:

1. Ever been judged or condemned?

   _____

   _____

   _____

   _____

   _____

2. What acts did you commit?

   _____

   _____

   _____

   _____

   _____

3. Are you guilty of being a stone thrower?

___

4. Let's be mindful, how do we treat someone who's in the wrong? Do you need to make an apology?

___

# Day 28

# Living Among the Tombs, It Seems

*"And they came over unto the other side of the sea, into the country of the Gadarenes. And when he was come out of the ship, immediately there met him out of the tombs a man with an unclean spirit, who had his dwelling among the tombs; and no man could bind him, no, not with chains: because that he had been often bound with fetters and chains, and the chains had been plucked asunder by him, and the fetters broken in pieces: neither could any man tame him. And always, night and day, he was in the mountains, and in the tombs, crying, and cutting*

*himself with stones. But when he saw Jesus afar off, he ran and worshipped him, and cried with a loud voice, and said, What have I to do with thee, Jesus, thou Son of the most high God? I adjure thee by God, that thou torment me not. For he said unto him, Come out of the man, thou unclean spirit. And he asked him, What is thy name? And he answered, saying, My name is Legion: for we are many. And he besought him much that he would not send them away out of the country. Now there was there nigh unto the mountains a great herd of swine feeding. And all the devils besought him, saying, Send us into the swine, that we may enter into them. And forthwith Jesus gave them leave. And the unclean spirits went out, and entered into the swine: and the herd ran violently down a steep place into the sea, (they were about two thousand;) and were choked in the sea."*

~Mark 5:1-13

There is a spirit of depression that has been rampant and has captivated a lot of this generation. We have identified and witnessed it among people from different walks of life. It has affected the rich, the poor, the young, and the old, and whatever color, class, or creed, it has no respect of person. In the news, there have been reports of suicide, homicide, drug abuse, self-harm, alcohol addiction, insanity, and the list goes on in the name of depression. It's an evil spirit.

From the days of Jesus Christ, we see men who lost their minds, but Christ showed up. This specific text in Mark 5 tells about a man living among the tombs. He had to be bound hands and feet because of damages he would cause even to himself. This behavior has become common in today's world. We see similarities with him and people who are even close to us. We have identified it and likened it to some symptoms of depression. The spirit of depression will have you not eating, not showering; I've even heard of people who choose to stay in a dark room all day, not wanting to face the world. As my Pastor, Rebecca Stewart, would always say, "Consider what drove them to that place." People have been through some things in their lifetime, e.g., hurt, abuse, rape, molestation, abandonment, cursed out, rejection, and the list continues. The effects are significant.

In the base scriptures, we see this man who lived among the tombs, crying to Jesus Christ. First, he opened his mouth to acknowledge Christ and cry out for help. Depression can be compared to living among the tombs; it's cold, lonely, scary, and not good, but speak out. Talking will heal you. Not only just talking, but there's a man, the same Jesus Christ, who can make a difference in your life. Others may get tired of dealing with your behavior, so they'll bind you and leave you alone, not Jesus. He can permanently rebuke this spirit and chase it away (Philippians 2:10). Jesus heals, delivers, and sets free; there's nothing too hard for him to do.

I once shared a story that I heard of a man advised to place a chair by his bedside so Jesus could sit and he could talk to him. The man did it, and he continually spoke to that chair, believing Christ was sitting there, and he did it and was relieved of what was going on with him. He maintained that practice until the day he was found sitting on his bed with his head on the chair seat. We can conclude that he died peacefully with his head in Jesus's lap. Try the empty chair therapy and talk it out, but just know that Jesus is always sitting right there listening to your cares.

# *Reflections:*

1. Have you ever been depressed, or are you still?

   _____

   _____

   _____

   _____

   _____

   _____

2. How do you deal with your depression when it comes on?

   _____

   _____

   _____

   _____

   _____

   _____

3. Have you tried talking or crying out to someone?

___

4. Have you tried talking to the Lord? Go, Get that chair!

___

# Day 29

# *You Are an Important Member*

*"For as the body is one, and hath many members, and all the members of that one body, being many, are one body: so also is Christ. For by one Spirit are we all baptized into one body, whether we be Jews or Gentiles, whether we be bond or free; and have been all made to drink into one Spirit. For the body is not one member, but many.*

*~1 Corinthians 12:12-14*

Once you are alive, and you belong to a group, you are a member of a body. It may be a public body, a professional body, a family, a community, a church, etc., you are a part of that body, and you help complete it.

Now, as we can all see, the body comprises different parts, such as the head and the neck. The hands, the torso, the loins, the legs, the feet, and other members are hidden inside, so they are not visible to natural eyes unless scanned by specific machines. However, some of these hidden members are essential to the body's functioning.

So what, you may ask, does this has to do with us as individuals? As the different body members have their individual purposes, so are each of us in our respective bodies (church, school, family, etc.). You may be the head of your body, and you have to be attended to daily, so there's a sense of appreciation, love, and respect. Knowing you are the brain that leads is itself deserving of all due respect and honor.

But what about you being a member that is not always seen, you may be hardly spoken of or addressed, does it make you any less? It does not. You are just as needed as the eyes, the nose, and the mouth. As a matter of fact, you may even be more important than some members who can be seen easily because some members, such as the hands or the feet, can be replaced or the family can live without. Still, some hidden members are needed to live, for example, the heart, the lungs, and the kidneys. Let's take the heart, for example, it is on the inside of the body, not seen, but without a heart, that body is dead. You may want to consider yourself as your body's heart, knowing it can't continue without you. You might get treated as a small toe, not much attention given, but without you, there is an imbalance, loss of strength, and gout. You might be treated as other sections that are not readily spoken about, but without you, the body cannot function to its fullest capacity (1 Corinthians 12:22-24). So, whatever member of the body you may see yourself as, know that you are essential and needed to survive.

As members, we must function in our respective places and work with each other as members are dependent on each other to have an entire effective and productive body.

# *Reflections:*

1. As what member of the body do you see yourself?

_____

_____

_____

_____

_____

_____


2. Do you consider yourself essential to the body you belong to?

_____

_____

_____

_____

_____

_____

3. How can you improve your function?

_____

_____

_____

_____

_____

_____

_____

# Day 30

# Rejected – Now Needed...

*"The stone which the builders refused
Is become the head stone of the
corner."*

*~Psalm 118:22*

In the Bible, the book of Judges, Chapter 11 to be exact, there is a story of a man named Jephthah who was the son of a harlot. Because of who Jephthah's mother was, he was rejected by his very own brothers, who treated him as nothing (Day 5 Devotional). He was, therefore, cast out of his own land and had to find refuge in another but in his new dwelling place, he was loved and respected. There came a time when his land of origin came under attack from the enemy, and it seemed hopeless for them as they were facing a mighty army. It was in this desperate moment that Jephthah's brothers remembered him because he was a strong man and one who could fight. Jephthah's brothers had rejected him, but when trouble arose, he was needed and indeed was the one who, by the help of God, delivered them from the hands of the enemy. He led them to victory.

Some of us, like Jephthah, had been rejected or not counted as necessary because of different reasons. Some, because of family, our past, jealousy, stature, etc., have been denied access to what rightfully belongs to us. Here, we see where this young man went through it all to the point of being cast out of his own inheritance, but there's a God who sits high and looks low. He rules in the affairs of men (Daniel 4:17), so he gives to whomever he will and sets up those we least expect to lead. God has the final say in our lives; therefore, no man can stop what God has in store for us.

God will allow your enemies who rejected you to become dependent on you. Husband, wife, siblings, parents, or friends you love with your whole heart may turn their backs on you and are ungrateful to you, but just keep doing good. Remember, the seed you sow will be harvested (Day 26 Devotional). Joseph was rejected and sold out by his brothers (Genesis 37) because of jealousy. It all worked out for them because they had to depend on him for food to survive. Also, Jesus was rejected, despised, abused, and mistreated. Still, He was the sacrificial lamb that has become our savior and Lord today. The stone that the builders rejected had become the headstone of the corner.

You felt cast off and rejected, but very soon you'll be needed... you are that member that the body cannot function without (Day 29 Devotional). When you become that needed piece, remain humble and demonstrate unconditional love.

# *Reflections:*

1. How have you handled rejection in the past?

_____

_____

_____

_____

_____

_____


2. What made you feel rejected?

_____

_____

_____

_____

_____

_____

3. Was it more destructive based on who the rejection came from?

_____
_____
_____
_____
_____
_____

4. Do you see yourself already as a cornerstone? How do you react to those who once rejected you?

_____
_____
_____
_____
_____
_____

# Day 31

# *Different Seasons... Different Times*

*"To every thing there is a season, and a time to every purpose under the heaven: a time to be born, and a time to die; a time to plant, and a time to pluck up that which is planted; a time to kill, and a time to heal; a time to break down, and a time to build up; a time to weep, and a time to laugh; a time to mourn, and a time to dance; a time to cast away stones, and a time to gather stones together; a time to embrace, and a time to refrain from embracing; a time to get, and a time to lose; a time to keep, and a time to cast*

*away; a time to rend, and a time to sew; a time to keep silence, and a time to speak; a time to love, and a time to hate; a time of war, and a time of peace."*

*~Ecclesiastes 3:1-8*

---

There are four seasons in each year. Different climates distinguish a season. These four are Spring, Summer, Fall/Autumn, and Winter. Each season has its purpose and effect on the earth. In spring, we see trees, leaves, and flowers birthing, and a freshness lingers, telling us things are in bloom. Everything becomes bright and beautiful with the frequent showers of rain. Then, there's summer, when it gets warm and very sunny. There is an atmosphere of fun, life, and excitement; people are out and about. Vacations are at their peak, and people are making the most of it, especially if living in countries that experience lousy winter weather. Autumn that time when all these beautiful leaves and trees begin to change. It is lovely when you admire the leaves in different colors and shades, getting ready to fall off the trees as the temperatures get cooler. Things begin to dry up, and then we feel winter coming in. It starts to get dark very early in the daytime and gets icy cold; things seem a bit lifeless as the bitter cold sweeps in. Some folks will even experience snowfall during this season.

What do the seasons have to do with life, though? Well, just as there is time for every season, there is time for everything in this walk of life. Our lives come with seasons, as do the years. We can compare these seasons to the different stages of life.
- Spring - Time of birth,
- Summer - Youthful and active years,
- Autumn - Season of life where you begin to change
- Winter years – Fading into death

Some will not experience the entire season in their lifetime. Still, however long we survive, it is important to know what we do with our time. Time is vital. In the book of Ecclesiastes,

Chapter 3 clearly outlines a time for every thunder under the sun. A time to laugh and cry, a time to plant and harvest, a time to be born and die. Different seasons and times come with different challenges. It's to make us aware that our lives will never be the same constantly; there will always be ups and downs.

Whatever season we are in, it pays for us to embrace the moment and learn the lessons that each phase may bring cause it's only for a time. It will not last. We also have to be able to identify our seasons so that we do not miss out on the blessings that accompany them. Don't be harvesting when it's planting season and vice versa. Don't be crying when it's laughing time. Don't be killing when you should be made alive. Be aware.

Now is a time for us to be living for Christ. If you haven't accepted him yet, now is the time to do so (2 Corinthians 6:2). Don't wait until it's too late when time is no more. The next moment is not guaranteed.

# Reflections:

1. Do you know what season you are in?

   _____

   _____

   _____

   _____

   _____

   _____


2. What actions are you taking to result in a good season?

   _____

   _____

   _____

   _____

   _____

   _____

3. Are you embracing your season? If not, why?

_____

_____

_____

_____

_____

_____


4. How productive or successful was your prior season?

_____

_____

_____

_____

_____

_____

# *About the Author*

Stadene Campbell is an Assistant Pastor of a church family in Brooklyn, New York, known as Come As You Are Healing and Deliverance Center. She is originally from a small town in Jamaica called Ewarton, St. Catherine, where she spent her early education years.

Growing up in the Caribbean wasn't easy for her. She was not born with a silver spoon in her mouth, which led to some life challenges. Nonetheless, these challenges led her to become the faithful woman of God she is today.

Stadene grew up with her grandmother, for the most part, who ensured the regular church services and good Sunday School attendances. At the same time, her mom worked out of town and sometimes overseas, and her dad lived separately and received the occasional visits. Stadene migrated for a few years to the UK., where she pursued a career in early childhood education. Living recklessly with no fear for God, she was no saint. Still, after a few mishaps, she returned to her homeland, where she got converted and dedicated herself to a life of Christianity. She spent some years going through a few struggles, including the loss of her mom, before migrating to the USA. Her previous lifestyle had left her with experiences that brought her to be humble before the Lord. Through prayers, fastings, and reading of the word, she got revelations and inspirations which birthed this book.

As she shares these divine inspirations, may your lives be changed, and may you have that HOLY GHOST encounter needed for deliverance, transformation, and upliftment.

www.ingramcontent.com/pod-product-compliance
Lightning Source LLC
LaVergne TN
LVHW021958060526
838201LV00048B/1614